PRESIDENTS *and* FIRST LADIES

GEORGE W. & LAURA
BUSH

By

Ruth Ashby

WORLD ALMANAC® LIBRARY

Please visit our web site at: www.worldalmanaclibrary.com
For a free color catalog describing World Almanac® Library's list of high-quality books
and multimedia programs, call 1-800-848-2928 (USA) or 1-800-387-3178 (Canada).
World Almanac® Library's fax: (414) 332-3567.

Library of Congress Cataloging-in-Publication Data

Ashby, Ruth.
    George W. & Laura Bush / by Ruth Ashby.
      p. cm — (Presidents and first ladies)
    Includes bibliographical references and index.
    ISBN 0-8368-5693-7 (lib. bdg.)
    ISBN 0-8368-5699-6 (softcover)
    1. Bush, George W. (George Walker), 1946-—Juvenile literature. 2. Bush, Laura Welch, 1946-—Juvenile literature.
3. Presidents—United States—Biography—Juvenile literature. 4. Presidents' spouses—United States—Biography—
Juvenile literature. I. Title.
    E903.A84   2004
    973.931'092'2—dc22
    [B]   2004047978

First published in 2005 by
World Almanac® Library
330 West Olive Street, Suite 100
Milwaukee, WI 53132 USA

Copyright © 2005 by World Almanac® Library.

Produced by Byron Preiss Visual Publications Inc.
Project Editor: Kelly Smith
Photo Researcher: Larry Schwartz
Designed by Four Lakes Colorgraphics Inc.
World Almanac® Library editorial direction: Mark J. Sachner
World Almanac® Library editor: Jenette Donovan Guntly
World Almanac® Library art direction: Tammy West
World Almanac® Library graphic designer: Steve Schraenkler
World Almanac® Library production: Jessica Morris

Photo Credits: AP/Wide World Photos: 12, 14, 15, 22, 26, 27, 29, 30, 31, 33, 37, 42 (top and bottom);
Classmates.com: 13; CORBIS: 20 (bottom), 23, 24, 28, 35; Federal Bureau of Investigation: 38;
George Bush Presidential Library: 5, 6, 7, 8, 9, 10, 16, 17, 18, 19, 20 (top), 21; NOAA: 32; Susan
Sterner/The White House: 4 (bottom), 36; The White House: 4 (top); U.S. Department of
Defense: 34, 40; U.S. Navy photo by Photographer's Mate 3rd Class Lewis Hunsaker: 39

Printed in the United States of America

1 2 3 4 5 6 7 8 9 08 07 06 05 04

CONTENTS

Words that appear in the glossary are printed in
boldface type the first time they occur in the text.

INTRODUCTION ★ ★ ★ ★ ★ ★ ★ ★ ★ ★

On September 17, 2001, President George W. Bush spoke to reporters and employees at the **Pentagon**, the headquarters of the U.S. Department of Defense, about the war on **terrorism.** Just six days earlier, on September 11, **Islamic** terrorists had hijacked four passenger planes and deliberately crashed one into the Pentagon and two into both towers of the World Trade Center in New York City. The fourth plane, perhaps bound for the White House, had crashed in a field in Pennsylvania. With the nation still reeling from the attacks, Bush and his national security team were making plans to retaliate. Already, it was apparent that terrorist leader Osama bin Laden and his fanatical **al-Qaeda** organization were behind the assault.

George W. Bush, forty-third president of the United States, in an official White House photo.

"Do you want bin Laden dead?" a reporter asked.

"They used to put up a wanted poster in the old West, as I recall, that said, 'Wanted Dead or Alive,'" Bush replied.

Bush said later that he meant to express "a bit of bravado," but many people thought the remark was too aggressive and over the top.

His wife, Laura Bush, was one of them. "Bushie, you gonna git 'em?" she teased him afterward. He did not, she warned him, sound very statesmanlike.

From the beginning of their relationship, quiet, calm Laura had steadied her more excitable, impulsive husband. "She's no shrinking violet," George once remarked. "If I do something she thinks needs to be toned down, she'll tell me." Now that America was in crisis, he could depend as always on her cool head and soothing presence. Together, they would try to present a united, resolute model for the nation.

"The best decision I ever made was asking Laura to marry me," George would repeat. "I'm not sure the best decision she ever made was saying yes. But I'm glad she did."

Laura Bush, first lady of the United States, in the White House Red Room.

THE LIFE OF THE PARTY

George Walker Bush likes to think of himself as a true Texan, a native son of spacious skies and wide-open range. Yet he is also the heir of a blue-blooded Connecticut family. He spent much of his youth and young adulthood in the ivy-covered schools and clubs of the eastern establishment. His life and his politics have been shaped by the tension between his family's roots and his own upbringing.

George W. is the oldest son of George Herbert Walker Bush and Barbara Pierce Bush. His father traces his lineage back to the British royal family, making him a very distant cousin of Queen Elizabeth II. As son of Connecticut senator Prescott Bush, George H. W., nicknamed Poppy, had a privileged youth in Greenwich, Connecticut, and Kennebunkport, Maine, where he grew up playing tennis, golf, and ping-pong with his five fiercely competitive siblings. He pushed himself to succeed, becoming captain of the baseball and soccer teams and president of his senior class at Phillips Academy, a prestigious private boarding school in Andover, Massachusetts.

George, called Georgie, all decked out in a cowboy outfit, riding a pony, c. 1950.

When he graduated, the United States was fighting World War II, and he became the youngest fighter pilot in the Naval Air Force. On September 2, 1944, George H. W. was shot down by Japanese antiaircraft fire just south of Japan and was rescued by an American submarine. Bush was the only man in his unit to survive.

Back home, the war hero married his sweetheart, Barbara Pierce, a lively and outspoken girl who was a descendant of the fourteenth president, Franklin Pierce. Together the two moved to New Haven,

Little Georgie sitting on his father's shoulders at Yale University, April 10, 1947.

Connecticut, where Bush enrolled at his father's alma mater, Yale University. In New Haven, on July 6, 1946, their first child was born: George Walker Bush. After graduating with highest honors, Poppy decided to try his luck in the oil business. He, Barbara, and little Georgie went west, drawn, he said later, by the "romance and adventure of searching for black gold."

Texas Boyhood

After a few years, the young family found itself smack in the middle of west Texas, in an oil boomtown called Midland. During the 1950s, when rows of oil **derricks** stretched to the horizon, Midland became a destination for displaced Easterners who wanted to strike it rich. By the end of the decade, it would be the wealthiest town, per capita, in the nation. The Bushes fit right in and so did their growing family: Pauline Robinson "Robin" Bush, born in 1949; and John Ellis "Jeb" Bush, born in 1953. George W. loved everything about the wide-open, dusty country, especially ponies and cowboy boots. Georgie had "grown to be a near-man," Poppy wrote his father. "He talks dirty once-in-awhile, and occasionally swears, aged four and a half."

Then, tragedy struck. One day, Barbara noticed that three-year-old Robin was acting listless and tired. When she rushed her daughter to a doctor, he diagnosed Robin with leukemia, a then-incurable blood disease. For the next six months, the Bushes flew back and forth between Midland and New York City, where Robin was treated at the Memorial Sloan-Kettering Institute, famous for its cancer treatments. Although Georgie knew his sister was ill, he did not know the disease was life threatening.

When his parents came to pick him up at Sam Houston Elementary School in October 1953, George W.

Bush family portrait, 1956. Clockwise from top right: George H. W. Bush holding Neil; Barbara holding Marvin; Jeb; and George W.

was surprised to see that his little sister was not in the car. "Where's Robin?" he asked.

Somberly, they told him that she had died. At first it was all too much for the little boy to take in. "Why didn't you tell me she was so sick?" he asked over and over. Forty years later, George W. could still remember his shock. "Those minutes remain the starkest memory of my childhood," he wrote, "a sharp pain in the midst of an otherwise happy blur."

As Barbara Bush struggled to recover, Georgie became his mother's comforter and companion. One day his mother heard him tell a friend, "I can't leave my mom alone. She needs me," Barbara realized she was leaning too much on her seven-year-old son. That moment, she remembered later, she began her cure. Over the years, George would have three more siblings: Neil Mallon, born 1955; Marvin Pierce, born 1956; and Dorothy Walker, born 1959. As he grew older, George W. would gain several nicknames to distinguish

George W., age eight, in his Little League uniform, spring 1954.

him from his father: Junior (he wasn't really), Shrub, Dubya (the Texan pronunciation of *W*), and Bushie.

George W. has always said that Midland was the perfect place to grow up. It "was a small town with small-town values," he remembered. It was the sort of town where parents looked out for other people's children. And that was just as well, because energetic Georgie was always in some sort of trouble.

George was the class clown, forever making comments and rude noises from the back of the room. Once he was sent to the principal's office for drawing a mustache, side-burns, and a goatee on his face, and once he hit a baseball through a neighbor's window. George wasn't much of a reader and never excelled in school, but he loved sports, especially baseball, and played enthusiastically on the local Little League team. "Georgie aggravates . . . me at times (I am sure I do the same to him)," his father wrote Prescott Bush when Georgie was ten, " but then at times I am so proud of him I could die. He is out for Little League—so eager . . . he has good fast hands and even seems to be able to hit a little."

Outgoing and popular, George was the president of his seventh-grade class at San Jacinto Junior High School. A year later, his father began another business venture near Houston, and the family moved. For the first time, George was sent to a private school, the exclusive Kinkaid School, where the friendly boy became popular immediately. After ninth grade, he found out he was being shipped far away, to attend his father's prep school in Andover, Massachusetts. "Man, what did you do wrong?" a classmate teased him.

An Eastern Education

It was a tough transition. "Andover was cold and distant and difficult," George W. remembered. "Forlorn is the best way to describe my sense of the place and my initial attitude." At first, he worried that he would flunk out. The first paper he wrote for English class came back marked 0, with the comment, "Disgraceful." George was clearly out of his league academically, but he worked hard not to disgrace the family. And he threw himself into his social life. Talkative and feisty, he became known as the Lip. As head cheerleader for the Andover team (the all-boys school had no female cheerleaders), he raised school spirit to an all-time high.

The ever-popular George W. at Yale University.

George's distinguished, wealthy alumni family helped earn him entry into his first choice of college— Yale. Later he would describe the class that entered Yale in 1964 as the "last in a long time to have short hair." Over the course of the decade, Yale, like many other college campuses, would be rocked by student unrest. George W.'s classmates staged **teach-ins** and **draft** card burnings to protest the unpopular **Vietnam War.** They grew their hair long, began wearing jeans, and questioned authority. In 1967, Yale would change its admissions procedures and start accepting more public school applicants and, in 1969, women.

The social revolution of the 1960s passed Bush by. None of his classmates remembers George W. as having any particular political interests while he was an undergraduate. He joined no political organizations and attended no debates or speeches. Of course, he always supported his father George H. W. Bush, who ran for the Senate on the **Republican** ticket in 1964—and lost. George W.'s conservative politics set him in opposition to the many leftist students and liberal professors at Yale. For his part, George W. grew to resent what he thought of as East Coast intellectual snobbism. "I always felt that people on the East Coast tended to feel guilty about what they were given," he said. "Everybody has been given free will, and everybody has the chance to succeed. If someone has failed economically, that does not mean that the rest of us should be judged differently."

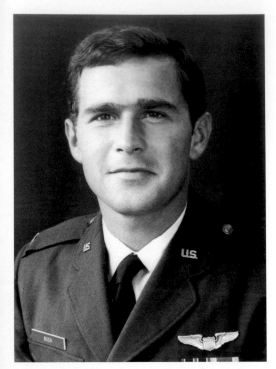

George W. Bush in his Texas Air National Guard uniform. George W. served in the Guard from 1968–1973.

George W. was not exceptionally interested in the academic side of college either. Bush was "not what I'd call a lover of reading," his old friend Joe O'Neill said. "He's just always on the go. Boom, boom, boom. And he has been since Day One. Nervous energy. I just don't see how he ever got through Yale. I mean, you have to read."

George W. was very social in college. He joined the Delta Kappa Epsilon fraternity, where he amazed his fellow members by naming all the pledges (new members) in the room. At DKE, George W. was the life of the party and the chief organizer of parties and sports events. DKE was a heavy-drinking fraternity with the biggest bar on campus, and George had no trouble keeping up. By his junior year, he was president of the fraternity. In his senior year, he was tapped for Yale's most prestigious secret society, Skull and Bones, to which his father and grandfather had also belonged.

The Nomadic Years

After graduation in spring 1968, George had a decision to make. The Vietnam War was still raging, and he was about to lose the student deferment from military service he had received while still a college student. Like many young men, he had little intention either of volunteering for an unpopular war or of being drafted for it. Instead, family connections enabled him to secure a coveted spot in the Texas Air National Guard. In his five-and-a-half years of part-time duty, he worked hard and played hard. He enjoyed flying F-102 fighter jets. One commander praised him: "Lt. Bush's skills far exceed his contemporaries. . . . He is a natural leader whom his contemporaries look to for leadership." When he wasn't flying, George was partying. Later he called these hard-drinking days his "nomadic years."

For nine months, he also worked at an inner-city youth

program in Houston called PULL (Professional United Leadership League). He was very good at working with young children and was appalled to see the rundown conditions in the ghetto. George later called the experience "tragic, heartbreaking, and uplifting, all at the same time." Years later, he was saddened to discover that one of his favorite boys had died young, shot on the Houston streets.

In 1973, he received an early discharge from the guard so he could attend Harvard Business School. Two years later, with a master's degree in business from Harvard under his belt, George W. decided, once again, to follow in his father's footsteps and enter the Texas oil business. He started from the ground up, literally, working as a "land man" researching the mineral rights of prospective oil properties.

George also wanted to emulate his father in another way and go into politics. To appeal to voters, friends told him, he had better leave his partying days behind him and settle down. At age thirty, George W. Bush was the only man he knew who was not married. That was about to change.

The Vietnam War

The Vietnam War was a regional war that turned into a big problem for the United States. It began in the late 1950s. At that time, Vietnam was divided into two nations: North Vietnam, controlled by **Communists**; and U.S.-supported South Vietnam. Presidents Dwight D. Eisenhower and John F. Kennedy sent military advisors to aid the South Vietnamese government in its fight against rebel Communist **guerrillas**. The United States believed that if Vietnam fell to the Communists, other Southeast Asian nations would topple too, like a row of dominoes. After Kennedy's assassination in 1963, the new president, Lyndon B. Johnson, sharply increased American involvement, sending combat troops and instituting a military draft. By the end of 1968, Johnson had sent more than half a million American troops to fight in a seemingly endless, and increasingly unpopular, war.

The war split America right down the middle. Pro-war "Hawks" insisted that America was fighting for freedom against international communism. Anti-war "Doves" argued that the war was unjust and that young men were being sent to die in a war the United States could not win. On college campuses across the country, students protested, burning their draft cards and staging sit-ins and marches.

By the summer of 1967, when George W. Bush was entering his senior year at Yale, 30,000 young men were being drafted into the military per month. Middle- and upper-class youths often found ways to avoid the draft through student deferments and other means. National Guard positions such as the one Bush obtained were highly sought after, as guardsmen were rarely sent to Vietnam. As a result, the burden of fighting and dying in the war fell heavily on young working-class and poor people.

The Vietnam War did not end for the United States until 1973, when President Richard Nixon pulled the last U.S. troops out. Two years later, North Vietnam overran the South. The war had caused more than 58,000 American deaths and had divided the nation.

A LOVER OF BOOKS

The little girl who would grow up to become George W. Bush's wife lived just twelve blocks from his boyhood home in Midland, in a one-story home that her father, Harold Welch, built himself. They never met as children, even though George and Laura attended the same junior high school in seventh grade. Fate, apparently, had something else in store.

Born on November 4, 1946, Laura was the only child of Harold Welch, a local builder, and his wife, Jenna. Laura was always aware that her parents were disappointed because they couldn't have more children, and she tried to make it up to them. "I wanted to be the best little girl I could possibly be," she told a friend. "I just wanted them to be happy with our little family." Pretty, bright-eyed Laura was a naturally cheerful and content child who loved dolls and animals. Like George, she had an amazing ability to remember people's names. She startled her mother by coming home at the end of the first week of nursery school and reeling off the names of all the kids in her class.

In Laura's hometown of Midland, Texas, a herd of buffalo edges up to an oil well. The picture was taken in 1947, the year after Laura was born.

Midland was a safe, almost idyllic, place to grow up. Like many other children, Laura attended church once a week and sang in the "cherub" choir. She took ballet and sewing lessons, and joined a Brownie troop. What set Laura apart from her classmates, however, was her passion for reading. She sped through Laura Ingalls Wilder's Little House books; *The Secret Garden*, by Frances Hodgson Burnett; and *Little Women*, by Louisa May Alcott. Already, by age seven, Laura had declared to her beloved second-grade teacher that she wanted to become a teacher.

Laura was straight A student in high school and also had a full social calendar. In Texas, where the driving age was fourteen, she and her friends would cruise around Midland in the family sedan. "There were at least five girls in the car every time we went out," a friend remembered. "We liked Kent cigarettes and would be down on the floor in the back of the car, smoking. We all stopped smoking eventually." Another friend described Laura as a "nice, very kind person. But that makes her sound boring, and she wasn't. She was also very outgoing, with a little mischievous streak. . . . You know the song 'Girls Just Want to Have Fun'? Well, that was Laura, too." Laura seemed to have a date for every dance and post-football game party. For a while in her junior year, she had a steady boyfriend, a popular athlete named Michael Douglas. By her senior year, the romance had cooled, but they were still good friends.

A Sudden Tragedy

On November 6, 1963, Laura and her friend, Judy Dykes, were out in the Welchs' Chevrolet, going east across the flat, nearly bare Texas plains. Deep in conversation, Laura didn't notice a stop sign and drove through it, crashing into the side of a Corvair sedan crossing in front of her. She and Judy screamed as the Chevrolet swerved into a ditch. As the Corvair spun around, its driver was fatally wounded and thrown from the car. The girls were taken to the hospital and released with just a few scratches. It was up to Harold Welch to tell his distraught daughter the bad news: The young man she had killed was her good friend, Michael Douglas.

Laura Welch's yearbook photo, Robert E. Lee High School, Midland, Texas, 1964.

For Laura, the accident was crushing. Devastated, she holed up in her room for weeks. "I grieved a lot," she remembered later. "It was a horrible, horrible tragedy. . . . It was a comeuppance. At that age, you think you're immortal, invincible. You never expect to lose anybody you love when you're so young."

While things were relatively quiet for Laura at SMU, other college campuses around the nation were heating up with antiwar demonstrations and student protests. At Kent State (above), Ohio National Guardsmen threw tear gas across the campus lawn at students protesting the war on May 7, 1970. The Guard killed four students and wounded nine.

The girl who came back to school that winter was more subdued. She graduated and went to Southern Methodist University (SMU), a college in an affluent section of Dallas. Though she was there during the turbulent 1960s, she missed the war protests and student demonstrations. SMU was a quiet, conservative place, where students went to fraternity parties and politics remained on the back burner. Laura joined a sorority and enrolled in elementary education classes. As the women's liberation movement heated up in the late sixties, she remained committed to elementary school teaching, a traditional woman's job.

Only toward the end of her college career did Laura think about other choices. After graduation in 1968, she surprised her father by telling him that he had "programmed" her to become a teacher. What if she wanted to be a lawyer instead? Harold Welch immediately said he would send her to law school. "I had to admit," Laura said later, "that I didn't want to be a lawyer. I wanted to be a teacher."

Choosing a Career

After graduation and a short trip to Europe, Laura found a job as a third-grade teacher in Dallas. Then for three years she taught second grade at the mostly African American John F. Kennedy Elementary School in Houston. The kids loved the pretty, young teacher. Later, Laura said that she "learned more from them than they did from me—most importantly, I think, about the dignity of every child." While in Houston, Laura lived in a popular singles

The Sixties

The sixties, a time of great turmoil and change, began with the civil rights protests of 1960 and the assassination of John F. Kennedy in 1963. In those years, many citizens began to question basic assumptions about race, sex, economic inequality, and social class in America. Black leaders such as Dr. Martin Luther King, Jr., protested racial **segregation** and discrimination in education, politics, housing, and employment. Women's rights leaders, such as Betty Friedan, demanded equality in jobs, pay, and education. Spokespeople for Native Americans, migrant workers, and other disadvantaged groups called for reforms and greater political power. Some Americans enthusiastically participated in the reform movements of the sixties, some strenuously opposed them, and many others were confused or sympathetic but basically uninvolved. The close of the Vietnam War signaled the end of the era of civil unrest, yet the changes wrought in those years still reverberate today.

At the conference "Women: A Political Force," women's rights activist Betty Friedan addresses the State Assembly in Albany, N.Y.

apartment complex called Chateaux Dijon. While Laura sunbathed by the pool, reading her books on the "quiet" side of the complex, hot-shot fighter pilot George Bush lived on the rowdy side, partying and playing volleyball. They never met.

Laura went back to school. She enrolled in the library science program at the University of Texas at Austin. Master's degree in hand, she embarked upon a new career as a children's librarian. Once again, she worked in a primarily minority school, this time in Austin. Many weekends, she drove the five hours back to Midland to visit her parents and old friends. By then she was thirty, still dating, but still unattached. All her married friends were eager to see her settle down.

One weekend, Laura Welch accepted an invitation to a barbecue that would change her life.

CHAPTER THREE

DEEP IN THE HEART OF TEXAS

For months, Laura's old elementary school friend Jan O'Neill had been begging her to come over and meet her husband Joe's friend George W. Bush, who was running for a seat in the local nineteenth congressional district.

Laura resisted. "I was so uninterested in politics," she said. "I thought he was someone real political, and I wasn't interested."

Finally on one hot August night in 1977, she agreed to stop by for a cookout. The minute George W. saw Laura, his mother said later, he was "struck by lightning." They chatted for hours, with George doing most of the talking. Laura was "gorgeous, good humored, quick to laugh, down-to-earth, and very smart," George recalled. "I recognized those attributes right away, in roughly that order." For her part, Laura went home that night and told her mother, "The thing I like about him is that he made me laugh."

Even the O'Neills were surprised that their matchmaking had worked. Calm, centered Laura seemed worlds away from wild, impulsive George, but their personality differences complemented each other, and their deep Texas roots gave George and Laura a lot in common. Also, the timing was right. They were both in their early thirties, ready to settle down and have children. After an intense, whirlwind courtship that lasted five weeks, George asked Laura to marry him.

In October, they went to Houston to meet his family. George W. introduced Laura to his paternal grandmother, Dorothy Walker Bush, whom Barbara Bush called the "single most competitive human being."

George W. Bush and Laura Welch's wedding, November 5, 1977. From left to right: Marvin Bush; Dorothy Bush; Neil Bush; Jeb Bush and his wife, Columba; Laura and George W.; Barbara and George H. W. Bush; and George H. W.'s mother, Dorothy Walker Bush.

"And what do you do?" Dorothy asked Laura, expecting to hear about her tennis or golf game.

"I read," Laura said. "And smoke." Barbara Bush remembered, "Mrs. Bush darn near collapsed. "

The November 5 wedding was small, with only seventy-five invited guests. Instead of a bridal gown, Laura wore a dress of off-white crepe-de-Chine fabric, with white gardenias at her waist and white pearls. Afterward, the newlyweds moved into George's beige brick ranch house in Midland—and went on the road. In fall 1977, George, emulating his father's political career, was working hard to win the Republican nomination for the local congressional seat.

Newlyweds George and Laura campaigning from the back of a pickup truck, 1978.

Becoming a Family

They got to know each other on the road. "It was a wonderful way to spend our first year of marriage," George remembered. "We were united on a common mission; we spent lots of time together." When she realized she was going to marry a politician, Laura made George promise her just one thing—that he would never make her give a speech. Almost immediately, he broke his word. Two months after they were married, he asked his wife to substitute for him at a rally in Levelland, Texas.

Laura climbed the courthouse steps and began. "When we were married, my husband said he'd never make me give a speech. So much for political promises." Then her voice trailed off, as she realized she didn't know what else to say. It was a difficult initiation for a woman who would later become a smooth, accomplished public speaker.

George won the Republican nomination, but in November 1978, he lost the election to the **Democratic** challenger, Kent Hance.

17

George W. Bush congressional
campaign poster, 1978.

Disappointed, George went back to Midland to manage his own oil
company, called Arbusto, the Spanish word for "bush." He had no
trouble convincing investors, usually friends of the family, to lend
him money. When he dug his first oil wells, however, they came up
dry. It was going to be harder for George W. than it had been for his
father to make it big in the oil business.

George and Laura both looked forward to starting their own
family, but after more than three years of marriage, Laura still hadn't
conceived. Discouraged, they had already registered at an adoption
agency when they discovered that Laura was pregnant—with twins!

From the beginning, Laura was told it was a high-risk pregnancy.
By her sixth month, she had developed toxemia, which is pregnancy-
related high blood pressure that can lead to swelling, kidney failure in
the mother, and distress for the baby. Seven weeks before the babies

were due, she was rushed to the hospital for an emergency delivery. However, Laura was stubborn. She knew that each day they spent inside the womb increased the babies' chance of being born healthy. So she held on—for two more nerve-wracking weeks.

Finally, on November 25, 1981, Laura Bush gave birth to two beautiful little girls, fraternal twins named Barbara and Jenna, after their grandmothers.

"It was such a resolute, powerful statement of motherhood," George said of Laura's determination, years later. The experience gave him a renewed respect for his wife. "She loves our daughters more than anything. She would lay her life down for them, and nearly did at birth."

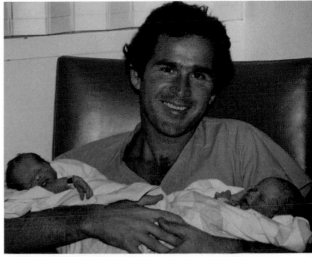

The jubilant father cradles his twin daughters, Barbara and Jenna, two hours after they were born on November 25, 1981.

Business Ups and Downs

Laura settled down to being what she had always wanted to be— a full-time mother. George struggled to make his company turn a profit. Arbusto, people began to joke, was really "Are Busted." He changed the name to the more staid Bush Exploration and tried to raise more money, but in the early 1980s, oil prices were low and investors scarce. Finally, George was forced to merge with a company named Spectrum 7. In return, he retained the chairmanship of the company. Oil prices continued their downward plunge, falling from nearly $100 a barrel in 1981 to $10 a barrel in 1985. Harken Oil and Gas saved Spectrum 7 by purchasing it before it was about to go bankrupt. The sale left Bush with a consulting fee of $120,000 per year, $600,000 in stock, and a seat on the board of directors.

George W. had landed on his feet—but only by drawing on family friends and connections. "I'm all name and no money," he was heard to say. The comparison with his father, Big George, who was wildly successful in the oil business, could not have been more clear. By then, George H. W. Bush was vice president of the United

Barbara, Laura, George W., and Jenna Bush at Kennebunkport, Maine, August 23, 1987. Temperamentally, Barbara resembles her more reserved mother, while Jenna is a lot like her outgoing dad.

States under President Ronald Reagan. What could George W. do to equal his father's legacy?

George W. had another big problem—alcohol. Over the years, Bush's drinking had become excessive. And he was not a pleasant drunk. When intoxicated, Dubya would become loud and obnoxious, even lose his temper. Alcohol, he would say later, "magnified aspects of my personality that probably don't need to be larger than they already are. . . . I wasn't so funny when I drank. Just ask my wife." Laura repeatedly asked him to stop.

The turning point came in July 1986, at a party with old friends to celebrate everyone's upcoming fortieth birthday. The next morning George woke up with a horrible, head-pounding, gut-wrenching hangover. Then and there he made the decision: "I'm quitting drinking," he told Laura. As week after week went by, Laura started to believe him. George W. has been on the wagon ever since.

During this time, George also became more devoutly religious. In the summer of 1985, the famous preacher Reverend Billy Graham came to visit his family at their summer home in Kennebunkport,

The world-famous preacher Billy Graham in 1990.

Maine. In the course of those few days, George W. said, Graham "planted a mustard seed in my soul, a seed that grew over the next year. . . . And it was the beginning of a change in my life. I had always been a religious person. . . . But that weekend my faith took on new meaning." It was the beginning of a whole new spiritual life for George.

Take Me Out to the Ballgame

In 1987, with Republican president Ronald Reagan's two terms in office winding down, George H. W. Bush decided to run for president, and his first son took time out to work on the campaign. About that time, an old friend came to George W. with a tempting idea. The Texas Rangers baseball team was up for sale. Why not invest in it? George W., who had always loved baseball, jumped at the chance. After he saw his dad win the 1988 presidential election and be sworn in on January 20, 1989, George and Laura moved to Dallas, ready for a new life.

With his family contacts and savvy people skills, George W. was able to put together a group of investors to pay $86 million for the team. His own share of the money, $606,000, he raised by using his Harken stock as collateral on a loan. For his efforts, George would become managing general partner of the team and receive a 10 percent bonus, plus a generous annual salary. Finally, George had a high-profile job he loved.

For the next five years, he hung out at the ballpark. He estimated that he and Laura went to fifty to sixty games a year. When he took the ball club over, the Texas Rangers were a mediocre team with an aging stadium. George worked to infuse new energy and money into the team, chatting with the players and the fans, cultivating members of the media, and building a new state-of-the-art ballpark. The Rangers, their star pitcher Nolan Ryan, and George W. Bush grew steadily more popular. A friend has said, "Before the Rangers, I told [George] he needed to do something to step out of his father's shadow. Baseball was it." When George and his partners sold the team in 1998, he made $15 million and became independently wealthy.

In 1992, Arkansas governor Bill Clinton defeated George H. W. Bush in the presidential race. Big George's political career was over, and the torch had been passed. It was George W.'s turn. Dubya, it was decided, would run for governor of Texas.

President George H. W. Bush, baseball broadcaster Joe Morgan, and George W. Bush in the locker room of the Texas Rangers, April 8, 1991. A lifelong baseball fan, George W. really enjoyed his years as part owner of the Texas Rangers.

21

The Persian Gulf War

In August 1990, Iraqi dictator Saddam Hussein invaded nearby Kuwait, a small nation on the northern border of Saudi Arabia. Concerned that the oil fields of Saudi Arabia were threatened, President George H. W. Bush skillfully organized a large international coalition to cut off trade with Iraq. He also obtained the **United Nations'** (UN) permission to invade if Iraq didn't withdraw. On January 17, 1991, the coalition launched an air war that dropped more bombs in six weeks than had been dropped during all of World War II. A month later, just one hundred hours after the first ground troops were deployed, Iraq surrendered. President Bush decided not to push forward into Baghdad and capture Saddam, and a cease-fire was called on February 28. As commander in chief of a victorious army, Bush saw his personal popularity rating shoot up to 90 percent. Saddam, meanwhile, brutally suppressed rebellions in the south and north of Iraq, killing tens of thousands of **Shiite Muslims** and **Kurds.**

One of the provisions of the 1991 cease-fire was that Iraq would admit UN arms inspectors to ensure that Iraq had destroyed all its nuclear, chemical, and biological weapons. In 1997, Saddam threw all the American members of the team out of the country. After much arm-twisting, Iraq agreed the following year to cooperate with the inspectors but went back on its word. By 2001, it was still refusing to let inspection teams in. Many intelligence and foreign policy experts took this as probable evidence that Saddam was rebuilding Iraq's weapons arsenal.

U.S. Marines patrol near a burning oil well outside Kuwait City after the Persian Gulf War, March 7, 1991.

PLUNGE INTO POLITICS

The Texas governor's race pit George W. against a popular Democratic **incumbent,** Ann Richards. For George, the contest was personal. Richards had first burst onto the national scene by giving the keynote speech at the Democratic **National Convention** in 1988. George H. W. Bush, she joked, had been "born with a silver foot in his mouth." George just couldn't forgive someone who made fun of his father.

Ann Richards campaigned against George W. in the Texas gubernatorial election of 1994.

At first, Laura wanted to make sure that George W. wasn't running just because he had something to prove. George, though, was adamant that "I'm not running because I'm George Bush's son. I'm running because I'm Barbara and Jenna's dad." When Richards attacked him personally, belittling him with condescending nicknames like "Shrub" and "Junior" and talking about his political inexperience, Laura helped temper his response. Thanks to Laura's calming influence, George took the high road and didn't retaliate. Instead, he said, he would "kill her with kindness."

He also evaded reporters' questions about his wild youth, stressing instead his abstention from alcohol and his religious conversion. When asked whether he'd ever used drugs, Bush said, "Maybe I did, maybe I didn't—what's the relevance?"

Election day 1994 was a gala Republican election year for Texas. George W. swept into office with 54 percent of the vote.

First Family of Texas

George, Laura, and their thirteen-year-old daughters moved into the 140-year-old governor's mansion in Austin, once inhabited by Texas Republic president Sam Houston. Governor Bush pledged to work

An antideath penalty demonstrator protests against Texas governor George Bush.

together with the mostly Democratic **legislature.** Throughout his term, he tried to fulfill some of his campaign pledges: promoting local control of education, toughening laws on juvenile crime, reforming welfare, and protecting corporations from lawsuits. He earned criticism, too, from environmental groups for his probusiness legislation and from antideath penalty advocates for his record on executions. During Bush's five years as governor, Texas put to death 152 people, including the first woman in Texas to be executed since the Civil War.

Laura blossomed as First Lady of Texas. "Well," she said, "if I'm going to be a public figure, I might as well do what I've always liked doing—which means acting like a librarian and getting people interested in reading." The first thing she did was to sponsor a reading by Texas authors during the **inauguration,** and subsequently helped to establish an annual Texas Book Festival.

She also sponsored breast cancer awareness programs, started "Adopt-a-Caseworker" programs to help social service workers provide supplies for abused children, and supported the Texas Commission of the Arts. In 1996, House Bill 1640—known as Laura Bush's bill—put aside $215 million to promote reading instruction for young children. Years later, after her husband had been elected as president of the United States, *Time* magazine recognized her contributions to her native state: "Few can dispute that Laura Bush has been the best First Lady [of Texas] in years and years, maybe ever."

George was very proud of his wife's contributions. When he ran for reelection in 1998, he said, "There are many reasons I want people to reelect me as governor of Texas. The most important one may be to keep Laura Bush as our First Lady." He won a second term by a landslide, becoming the first Texas governor in history to earn two consecutive four-year terms.

Securing reelection was just the first step toward a more ambitious goal. Bush and his advisors were already talking seriously about a run for the presidency in 2000. First, though, he had to convince his family that this was the right thing to do. Laura was initially reluctant. She had had an inside look at her father-in-law's tough presidential campaigns and knew how wearing they could be on body and spirit. "I was worried about the impact on our family," she told reporters later. "I knew it would be hard to see someone I loved criticized."

The girls, though, begged their father not to run. Now high school seniors, they would be off to college in the fall of 1999. Studious, dark-haired Barbara, the twin who most resembled their mother, would attend her father's alma mater, Yale. Blonde, fun-loving Jenna, said to be more like George, would go to the University of Texas at Austin. Nether girl wanted the kind of publicity that came with being the child of a president. Who would want her every footstep dogged by Secret Service agents—even on a date?

Meanwhile, the political landscape was changing. In 1998, President Bill Clinton lied to the American people about his illicit relationship with an intern, Monica Lewinsky. He was **impeached,** though not convicted, by the U.S. Congress. Political analysts were sure that Vice President Al Gore, the probable Democratic candidate, would be tarnished by the scandal even though his own conduct was irreproachable. Republicans hoped that though the country was at peace, with a balanced budget and thriving economy, the Clinton scandal would hurt the Democrats' chances for reelection.

On the Campaign Trail

George W. Bush announced his candidacy in spring 1999. He would run, he said, as a "compassionate conservative." Like traditional conservatives, Bush favored personal responsibility, a strong national defense, tax cuts, and a smaller government, but the adjective "compassionate" was meant to highlight his sympathy for ordinary people. He advertised his fidelity to his wife to differentiate himself

Arizona senator John McCain, left, and Texas governor George W. Bush debate in South Carolina during the Republican nomination campaign, February 15, 2000.

from the irresponsible Clinton. "I'm going to bring honor, integrity, and dignity to the office," he told voters in Iowa.

Given his frat boy image and mediocre academic record, some people worried whether Bush was intelligent enough to become president. Matters weren't helped by his tortured syntax and misused words. His many mistakes were gleefully repeated by the media, but George had no trouble defending himself from charges of stupidity. "I know what I can do," he said, answering his critics. "I've never held myself out to be any great genius, but I'm plenty smart. And I've got good common sense and good instincts. And that's what people want in their leader."

Bush's main contender for the Republican nomination was Arizona senator John McCain, a decorated Vietnam veteran and moderate Republican. McCain traveled around the country on his campaign bus, the "Straight Talk Express," and connected so well with voters that he won the first primary in New Hampshire on February 1, 2000. Furious, George was about to blame his staff, but Laura looked him in the eye and said, "You've got to go out there, Bushie, and let people see that you're the better man for the job." Bush proceeded to defeat McCain in South Carolina, California, and New York and to regain the lead. The nomination was his.

Laura gave the kickoff speech at the Republican convention in Philadelphia. "They say parents often have to get out of the house when their kids go off to college because it seems so lonely," she joked. "Everyone deals with it in different ways. But I told George I thought running for president was a little extreme."

George W.'s Democratic opponent, Al Gore, was a policy expert known for his debating skills. Everyone said that George W. would be doing well if he just didn't make any mistakes. These low expectations worked to Bush's advantage. During the series of televised debates held before the election, George W. held his own, appearing relaxed and making no major mistakes.

Four days before the election, a story that Bush had kept under wraps for three decades was released. In 1976, he had been arrested for drunk driving in Kennebunkport. Yet after all the years of secrecy, it turned out that no one much cared about his youthful brush with the law. By the time the story came out, most people had made up their minds whom to vote for.

A Historic Election

Nothing could have prepared Bush or the American people for the roller coaster ride that was election night. First came the news that Michigan and Pennsylvania had gone to Gore, and that Gore and Bush were running neck and neck. At 7:47 P.M. eastern time, it seemed that Gore had won Governor Jeb Bush's own state of Florida, too. Television news announced that with Florida's twenty-five electoral college votes, the election was Gore's, but by 9:54 P.M., the networks had reversed themselves and declared that Florida was actually too close to call. At 2:15 A.M., the networks announced that Bush had won Florida after all.

Al Gore called to concede. "You're a good man," a jubilant Bush told him. Still, the Florida count went on.

More than an hour later, by 3:45 A.M., Bush's advantage was down to two hundred votes. Gore rang again and explained the situation. "Let me make sure I understand," George said in disbelief. "You're calling me back to retract your concession?"

"Well, there's no reason to get snippy," Gore replied.

By the morning after election day, George Bush had 246 electoral votes and Al Gore had 255. According to the U.S. Constitution, the presidency of the United States is not determined by popular vote, but by electoral college vote. The number of

Presidential candidates George W. Bush and Al Gore, right, exchange views during a debate at Washington University of St. Louis, October 17, 2000.

electoral votes for each state is determined by its number of U.S. representatives (based on that state's population) plus the senators from each state (always two). Whichever candidate wins a majority of votes in a particular state gets all of its electoral college votes. The magic number needed to win the national election is 270 votes. In other words, both Bush and Gore desperately needed Florida.

A manual recount of the votes was ordered by the Florida Supreme Court to address claims by Gore that some votes cast for him were not counted. Florida's punch-card ballots were confusing to voters and sometimes indecipherable even to the voting machines. For weeks, voting officials hand-counted ballots in three counties, trying to interpret the "chads," small pieces of the ballot that were punched out by the voter. Republican lawyers appealed the recount ruling to the **U.S. Supreme Court**, the highest court in the United States. On December 12, 2000, they announced their decision. By a vote of 5–4, the court overturned the decision of the Florida court. George Walker Bush would receive Florida's 25 electoral votes.

The final tally of the popular votes showed that Gore beat Bush 50,996,116 to 50,456,169—by over half a million votes. But the final electoral college vote was Bush 271, Gore 266. George Walker Bush would be the next president of the United States.

Laura Bush, George W. Bush, Barbara Bush, and former president George H. W. Bush in Austin, Texas, the day after the 2000 presidential election. They were still awaiting final election results.

TRIUMPH AND TERROR

Bush knew the election had divided the nation, and he promised to bring it together again. "I was not elected to serve one party, but to serve one nation," he said in his first televised address as president-elect on December 13. He had plenty to do before taking office in little more than a month, such as choosing a cabinet and preparing a policy agenda.

Laura also had to get used to her new role. On January 19, she admitted on the *Today* show that she disagreed with her husband about abortion laws. She did not think that *Roe v. Wade*, the Supreme Court decision that granted women the right to an abortion, should be overturned. Her statement alarmed right-to-life advocates, who were staunch Bush supporters. Later Laura apologized for "making a mess." She said, "I was not elected and George was, and I would never want to undermine him in any way." The incident taught Laura a lesson. From then on, she refused to tell reporters when she disagreed with her husband.

George W. Bush takes the oath of office as Jenna, Laura, and Barbara Bush (her head is hidden behind Chief Justice William Rehnquist) look on.

A Conservative Presidency

On January 20, 2001, Laura, Jenna, Barbara, and the rest of the Bush family stood with George W. Bush as he took the oath making him the forty-third president of the United States. His inaugural address called for "civility, courage, compassion, and character." That evening, the new "first couple" made the rounds of nine inaugural balls, dancing for less than a minute at each before moving on to the next. Laura was decked out in a stunning, bright red beaded gown and a ruby and diamond necklace.

The new president and first lady step out at one of the nine balls held to celebrate the Bush inauguration, January 20, 2001.

The Bushes settled into the White House and tried to make it their own. For the Oval Office, George retrieved the huge desk used by John F. Kennedy. For her part, Laura brought Jackie Kennedy's favorite red velvet chairs up from the storage rooms for the upstairs living quarters.

They set a schedule, waking by 5:00 A.M. and having coffee in bed while looking over the day's newspapers. By 7:00 A.M., George was in the office. For an hour a day, he worked out in the East Wing Gym. And, despite her packed appointment calendar, Laura tried to keep up with her reading. At night, she read in bed, mostly modern fiction, biographies, and southwestern authors. Lights out came at 10:00 P.M.

To truly relax, the Bushes went back to their new 1,600-acre (648-hectare) ranch in Crawford, Texas. They knew, when George ran for president, that they would need someplace to escape to. Laura put the finishing touches on the small, beautifully designed, one-story house during her husband's first months in office. There she would garden and he would fly-fish and cut brush.

First on Bush's policy agenda was a tax cut, which he presented to Congress shortly after the inauguration. Clinton's budget office had projected a $184 billion surplus for 2001, yet as the spring progressed, the stock market plunged and the economy began to go into a decline. Even though the surplus was almost gone by summer, Bush stubbornly insisted on his tax cut, insisting that it would stimulate economic growth. Congressional Democrats pointed out that most of the cut was targeted at the wealthiest Americans and would do little to help the hard-pressed middle or lower classes.

Bush caused consternation among America's foreign allies when he announced that the United States would violate the 1972 **Antiballistic Missile Treaty** by funding a program to build a shield against intercontinental ballistic missiles. He also dismayed the international community when he withdrew the United States from the Kyoto Protocol, an agreement to reduce atmospheric pollutants.

He thought that adhering to the terms of the agreement would hurt U.S. business.

In spring 2001, Laura made the list of *People* magazine's 50 Most Beautiful People. "She just seems fresh and warm and really lovely," the magazine said.

That same month, Yale University gave George an honorary degree. The president spoke at the graduation ceremony, joking about his own less-than-stellar academic record. "To

Laura Bush enjoys one of her favorite activities, reading to children, during a celebration of National Library Week, April 3, 2001. Looking on is Baltimore Orioles shortstop Mike Bordick.

those of you who received honors, awards, and distinctions, I say, 'Well done.' And to the C students, I say, 'You, too, can be president of the United States.'"

The Bushes' nineteen-year-old daughters were faring less well in the spotlight. On May 29, they were cited at a Tex-Mex restaurant in Austin for underage drinking. They were charged with a misdemeanor and ordered to pay a fine and do community service. This was Jenna's second alcohol-related offense in a year, and the Bushes were concerned. They made the girls promise not to drink in a bar until they were twenty-one.

The family enjoyed the month of August at the ranch. On September 8, 2001, Laura Bush hosted the National Book Festival in Washington, D.C. Three days later, she was scheduled to speak to the Senate Committee on Health, Education, Labor, and Pensions about funding early childhood education.

America under Attack

The morning of Tuesday, September 11, Laura put on a tailored red suit for her visit to Congress. George was down in Sarasota, Florida, on a tour to promote his education program. That morning, he was scheduled to visit a second-grade classroom at the Emma E. Booker Elementary School.

Bush had just arrived at the school when his press secretary Ari Fleischer received word that a plane had crashed into the North

September 11

On the morning of September 11, 2001, American history—and the George W. Bush presidency—changed irrevocably. At 8:46 A.M., a hijacked American Airlines passenger jetliner crashed into the North Tower of the World Trade Center, in downtown New York City. It penetrated above the ninety-sixth floor, exploding in a burst of flame and smoke. Just sixteen and a half minutes later, a United Airlines plane slammed into the South Tower. Other suicide hijackers steered a third plane into the Pentagon. A fourth plane never reached its destination, smashing instead onto an empty Pennsylvania field after a group of passengers rushed the hijackers. It is thought its intended target was the White House or the Capitol in Washington, D.C.

The fires ignited by the 10,000 gallons (37,854 liters) of fuel contained in each plane pushed temperatures in the towers to a soaring 2,000 degrees Fahrenheit (1,093 Celsius) and melted the steel framework of the buildings. Millions around the world watched in disbelief as, one after another, the 110-story towers crumbled in a massive cloud of dust. Where once had stood the tallest buildings in New York City now loomed smoldering mountains of rubble.

It would take more than two years for the day's death toll to be finalized: 2,602 people killed in the Twin Towers; 125 in the Pentagon; and 265 in the four airliners, including 19 hijackers. As commentators noted, it was the deadliest day on American soil since the Civil War.

A view of Ground Zero, as the ruins of the World Trade Center are known, on September 14, 2001.

Tower of the World Trade Center in New York City. Bush thought it might be pilot error or a terrible accident.

He was listening to second-grade students read to him when his chief of staff, Andrew Card, appeared about ten minutes later, just after 9:03 A.M. Card bent down and whispered in the president's ear. "A second plane has just hit the World Trade Center," Card said. "America is under attack."

Meanwhile, Laura arrived at the Capitol and was hurried into the office of Massachusetts senator Edward Kennedy. Together they watched the horror unfold on TV and saw George address the nation from Booker's media center at 9:30 A.M. "We have had a national tragedy," the president told America. "Two airplanes have crashed into the World Trade Center in an apparent terrorist attack on our country. I am going to conduct a full-scale investigation and hunt down and find those folks who committed this act. Terrorism against our nation will not stand."

At Emma E. Booker Elementary School, Chief of Staff Andrew Card informs President Bush that America is under attack.

Laura, too, spoke to reporters at the Capitol. "Our hearts and prayers go out to the victims of this act of terrorism. . . . Parents need to reassure children everywhere in our country that they're safe."

After a third jet crashed into the Pentagon at 9:40 A.M., Laura Bush was rushed to a secure location in Secret Service headquarters. In New Haven, Connecticut, and Austin, Texas, Barbara and Jenna Bush were whisked away by Secret Service agents and removed to safety. By now Bush had boarded the presidential plane, Air Force One, and was on his way, he hoped, back to Washington. He called Vice President Dick Cheney, who had gone down into the emergency bunker beneath the White House.

"We're at war," Bush said.

CHAPTER SIX

A WARTIME PRESIDENCY

President George W. Bush spent much of the long, chaotic day of the attacks hopping from one Air Force base to another. Possible threats to Air Force One and the White House kept him from returning to Washington, D.C. Finally, at 4:30 P.M., he called to tell Laura he was coming home. "Thank God, Bushie," she said.

Over the next few days, the president and first lady joined the rest of the nation in mourning the victims and comforting the survivors. Laura organized a national prayer service at the Washington National Cathedral on Friday, September 14, which they attended together with former presidents Clinton, Bush, Carter, and Ford, and their wives. President Bush got up to address the congregation. "The conflict was begun on the timing and terms of others," he said somberly. "It will end in a way and at an hour of our choosing." At the end of the service, the cathedral rang with the inspiring chords of "The Battle Hymn of the Republic."

Laura and George W. Bush wave American flags during a memorial service on October 11, 2001, held in honor of those who perished in the terrorist attack on the Pentagon. Behind them, a military choir sings "God Bless America."

Later that day, Bush visited Ground Zero in New York. In an unscripted moment, he took a bullhorn to address the crowd of rescue workers at the site. "I can't hear you!" one man yelled out.

"But I can hear you," Bush shouted back. "The rest of the world hears you. And the people who knocked these buildings down will hear all of us soon!"

Immediately after the terror attacks, Laura wrote reassuring letters to schoolchildren across the United States. On Monday, September 17, the president asked his wife to go to the memorial service for the United Flight 93 plane that had crashed in Pennsylvania. "You are the ones they thought of in the last moments of life," she said to the passengers' families. "And I want each of you to know today that you are not alone. We cannot ease the pain, but this country stands by you."

On September 23, the *New York Post* praised Laura's demeanor during this difficult time. "When terror struck, Laura Bush . . . almost instantly became the First Mom, comforting and reassuring the entire nation."

Standing atop the rubble of the World Trade Center on September 14, 2001, President Bush addresses rescue workers through a bullhorn.

Targeting al-Qaeda

President Bush, meanwhile, was formulating a plan of action. Shortly after the attack, Central Intelligence Agency (CIA) director George Tenet confirmed that al-Qaeda, a Muslim terrorist group, was responsible for the attacks. The leader of al-Qaeda and mastermind of the September 11 attacks, Osama bin Laden, was holed up in the war-ravaged country of Afghanistan, from which his training camps dispatched terrorists throughout the world. Al-Qaeda was protected by the **Taliban** regime, the fundamentalist Islamic rulers of Afghanistan. In a meeting of the national security team at **Camp David** in Maryland on September 15, Bush's chief advisors debated what to do. Some wanted to move immediately against all nations that sponsor terrorism, including Iraq. Secretary of State Colin Powell argued that the international coalition would only support an attack on al-Qaeda and the Taliban in Afghanistan.

On September 20, 2001, President Bush spoke to a joint session of Congress and announced a global war on terrorism. He laid out what came to be known as the Bush Doctrine. "We will pursue nations that provide aid or safe haven to terrorism," he declared. "Every nation . . . now has a decision to make. Either you are with us, or you are with the terrorists." He envisioned strong, assertive American leadership in the world.

On October 7, the United States and Britain launched air strikes in Afghanistan. Twelve days later, U.S. **Special Forces** were sent in on the ground. The Bush administration was counting on anti-Taliban Afghan troops called the Northern Alliance to do most of the ground fighting in the war. By November 13, Northern Alliance forces had seized control of the capital, Kabul. It took another twenty-three days of hard fighting before the Taliban gave up their stronghold of Kandahar in the south. In two months, Operation Enduring Freedom had deposed the Taliban and routed al-Qaeda.

The United States had not, however, succeeded in finding Osama bin Laden. Even as a new chairman of the interim Afghan government was sworn in, American troops continued to search for bin Laden and his associates in a network of cave hideaways. Bush acknowledged that U.S. forces would probably be in Afghanistan for "quite a long period of time."

In her new, more public role, Laura spoke out about women's and children's rights. The Taliban had been

Laura Bush and National Security Advisor Doctor Condoleezza Rice (right) meet with the U.S.-Afghan Women's Council, July 16, 2003. Laura takes a keen interest in the welfare of women in Afghanistan.

especially repressive toward women, forbidding them to work outside the home or go to school. Laura took the opportunity to highlight the plight of women in Afghanistan in a radio broadcast on November 17. "Muslims around the world have condemned the brutal degradation of women and children by the Taliban regime," she pointed out. "In Afghanistan, we see the world the terrorists would like to impose on the rest of us."

Even though they had not caught bin Laden, Bush and his advisors felt that their first action in the war on terror had been a success. The American public agreed with them, awarding President Bush a 90 percent approval rating, up from 55 percent before September 11. In *Time* magazine, historian Michael Beschloss wrote, "A President must make sure that if he is getting the U.S. into a war, it is for a purpose that is worth it. Second, he must make sure that he tells the American people at the outset how costly this might be. In both cases I think Bush has done amazingly well."

President Bush, addressing the United Nations General Assembly on September 12, 2002, demands that Saddam Hussein cooperate with international arms inspectors to investigate possible **weapons of mass destruction** in Iraq.

The War in Iraq

Bush's **State of the Union Address** on January 29, 2002, identified the next front in the war: the Middle Eastern nation of Iraq. Along with North Korea and Iran, Bush charged, Iraq was one of the three members of the "axis of evil," countries with state-sponsored terrorism. Since 1979, Iraq had been led by Saddam Hussein, a brutal dictator who dreamed of dominating the Middle East. Bush's father, George H. W., had beaten Hussein in the Gulf War of 1991 but had stopped short of invading the capital city of Baghdad to capture Hussein. Now George W. wanted to finish the job his father had started.

Terrorism and al-Qaeda

Osama bin Laden, the architect of the September 11 attacks, was a Saudi multimillionaire who headed the international Muslim terrorist organization al-Qaeda, meaning "the base." For years, bin Laden had trained suicide bombers and other terrorists who targeted American and Western interests. They hated America's military and economic power, what they saw as its permissive lifestyle, its support of Israel, and the presence of U.S. troops in some Arab countries. Declaring a "jihad," or holy war, against the United States, bin Laden pledged to "kill Americans and plunder their money." Before September 11, al-Qaeda had set off bombs in the garage of the World Trade Center in January 1993, in U.S. embassies in Kenya and Tanzania in 1998, and on the battleship USS *Cole* in October 2000. The war in Afghanistan dispersed and weakened al-Qaeda but did not destroy it or end Muslim terrorist efforts to plan and carry out attacks against America and its friends and allies.

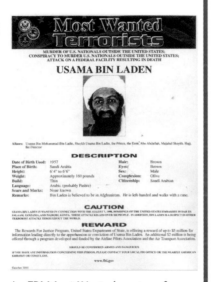

An FBI Most Wanted poster of Osama bin Laden, posted before September 11, 2001, states that bin Laden is wanted in connection with the bombing of U.S. embassies in Kenya and Tanzania in 1998.

As 2002 progressed, the president made clear his intention to pursue a "regime change" in Iraq. Other nations, such as old allies France and Germany, made it equally clear that they would not support a United States-led war in Iraq. In search of international consensus, Secretary of State Colin Powell urged taking the case to the United Nations.

On September 12, a day after the anniversary of the terrorist attacks, Bush spoke to the UN General Assembly and told them that they must force Saddam Hussein to destroy his weapons of mass destruction—illegal chemical, biological, or nuclear weapons. UN weapons inspectors began inspecting suspected sites for weapons but found nothing. Still, when Hussein issued a declaration stating that Iraq had no weapons of mass destruction, UN weapons inspector Hans Blix and Colin Powell said the statement exhibited a "lack of supporting evidence."

Preparations for war accelerated, as American troops continued to amass in the Persian Gulf. In the United States and around the world, antiwar demonstrators marched in the millions, but Bush pressed on, alleging in his State of the Union Address on January 28, 2003, that Hussein possessed both weapons of mass destruction and connections to al-Qaeda terrorists. Powell backed him up in a presentation at the UN in early February. When it became clear that the Security Council would nonetheless not vote to authorize military action, Bush decided to act without its approval.

On March 19, 2003, the first bombs were dropped in Iraq. Major military action lasted only three weeks. Resistance melted away, and American troops rolled into Baghdad. The regime had been overturned. On April 9, the world watched a group of U.S. Marines and Iraqi civilians topple a huge statue of Hussein in the capital, as the real Hussein went into hiding. On May 1, Bush made an appearance in his flight uniform on the deck of the aircraft carrier USS *Abraham Lincoln*. Behind him hung a huge banner that read MISSION ACCOMPLISHED.

Only it wasn't.

President Bush, dressed in a pilot's uniform, greets sailors on the aircraft carrier USS *Abraham Lincoln* prior to giving a speech announcing the end of major combat in Iraq.

CHALLENGES AHEAD

The war in Iraq, it turned out, was not over in May 2003. In some ways, the effort had just started. With the ousting of Saddam Hussein and his regime, the United States had become responsible for Iraq's reconstruction. And it became increasingly apparent to some experts that the Bush administration had not made adequate plans for the day after the fighting stopped.

The Iraq Dilemma

Iraqi dictator Saddam Hussein, immediately after his capture by American forces on December 13, 2003.

Iraq lay in ruins, with no government, no army, no police force, no schools, and no electricity. Its unemployment rate was at an astounding 75 percent. It would cost a lot more to get the country up and running than the administration had expected and, because it had alienated the UN and many old allies before the war started, nearly all of the expense would be borne by the United States. Bush was forced to return to Congress and ask for another $87 billion to reconstruct Iraq.

The human cost of the war kept rising, too. Attacks on Americans continued to increase, and soon the number of American casualties after active combat ended exceeded the number of casualties suffered during the war itself. By the end of April 2004, the tally was more than 700 American soldiers killed and more than 3,000 wounded.

The Bush administration was able to claim one significant victory. On December 13, 2003, Saddam Hussein was captured and taken into custody. The arrest was a big relief, but it did not alleviate the tensions within Iraq.

The most damaging problem, from the perspective of the Bush White House, was the inability to find any weapons of mass destruction in postwar Iraq. No matter where inspectors searched or whom they interviewed, weapons stockpiles remained invisible. Finally, on January 28, 2004, the former top inspector, David Kay, went before the Senate

Armed Services Committee and admitted, "We were all wrong. It is highly unlikely that there were large stockpiles of deployed militarized chemical and biological weapons" in Iraq. Nor had any definitive ties between Hussein and al-Qaeda been established, as Bush had alleged.

What had gone wrong? Had CIA intelligence been faulty? Or had Bush and his administration willfully exaggerated the weapons threat in order to make the case for war?

A Controversial President

Reacting swiftly, most Republicans insisted that the world was better off without Hussein in any case. Democrats, however, claimed that Bush had taken the nation to war under false pretenses. Suddenly George Bush found that he had a credibility problem. Steadfastly, he defended his actions. "Knowing what I knew then and knowing what I know today," he said, "America did the right thing in Iraq."

Then, there was the economy, which had slumped in 2001 and 2002 and had not yet fully recovered. More than 3 million jobs had been lost since the start of the Bush presidency, the largest loss since the administration of Herbert Hoover during the Great Depression. By early 2004, the economy was growing again, but few new jobs were being created.

The Patriot Act

Just forty-five days after September 11, 2001, Congress passed an antiterrorism law called the Patriot Act, which granted increased powers of surveillance and investigation to the FBI and other law enforcement agencies. President Bush signed it into law on October 26. Supporters hoped that it would give the United States new, vital tools to fight terrorism at home and abroad. Others worried that the act would seriously undermine civil liberties. One part of the bill, for instance, allowed both citizens and noncitizens to be imprisoned without formal charges. This change contradicted the constitutional guarantee of due process and equal protection under the law. Another part allowed the FBI to track book and Internet records in public libraries. Many claim that this was an invasion of the right to privacy.

As the 2004 presidential race heated up, Attorney General John Ashcroft pushed hard for the renewal of the Patriot Act in 2005. Critics noted that the Patriot Act was an emergency measure, passed with virtually no debate, and that it should not be renewed without a great deal of discussion. Keeping the homeland secure, they argued, should not mean giving up our hard-won civil liberties.

Protesters in Seattle, Washington, at an antiwar rally marking the one-year anniversary of the start of the U.S.-led war on Iraq.

First Lady Laura Bush and President George W. Bush in January 2004, the start of a reelection year.

In addition, the budget deficit was skyrocketing and estimated to climb to $521 billion in 2004. Many people blamed the deficit on Bush's tax cut plan, which would remove $947 billion from the budget over a five-year period.

As the United States headed into a new election year, voters were divided into two opposing camps: either they loved George W. Bush, or they hated him. Those who liked Bush admired his moral certainty, toughness, and willingness to act in defense of America's security. Those who disliked Bush thought him smug, stubborn, and dangerously simple-minded. Critics said he had taken the United States into an unnecessary war, jeopardized our foreign relations, and forced us into a debt so deep that it would be paid off by generations to come.

As the criticism grew, Laura stepped up to support her husband. Dignified and gracious, she was admired by many who thought George W.'s style was abrasive. In fall 2003, she traveled to France and Russia to help mend relations that had been strained by the war. Speaking before the United Nations Educational, Scientific and Cultural Organization (UNESCO) in Paris, she assured an international audience, "We believe in working with the nations of the world to promote the values shared by people throughout the world."

Back in the United States, she supported those causes that had always held her attention: women's health issues, programs in the arts, and education and reading initiatives. She also spoke at dozens of fund-raising luncheons and dinners, raising millions of dollars for the reelection campaign. "I'm very proud of the job that he's done," she said of her husband. "And I'm very proud of how steady he is." Impressed by her hard work and effectiveness, the reelection staff called Laura the "secret weapon" as Bush began his 2004 election campaign.

TIME LINE

1946	George Walker Bush born on July 6; Laura Welch born on November 4
1948	Bush family moves to Texas
1953	Pauline Robinson Bush (Robin) dies of leukemia on October 12
1959	Bush family moves to Houston, Texas
1961	George W. goes to Phillips Academy in Andover, Massachusetts
1963	Laura Bush in car accident that kills a friend on November 6
1964	George W. attends Yale University; Laura attends Southern Methodist University
1968	George W. graduates from Yale and joins the Texas Air National Guard; Laura starts job as third-grade teacher
1972	Laura earns master's degree in library science from the University of Texas in Austin and begins work as children's librarian
1973	George W. attends Harvard Business School
1977	George W. Bush and Laura Welch marry on November 5
1978	George W. loses election for a U.S. House of Representatives seat
1981	Jenna Welch and Barbara Pierce Bush born on November 25
1985	George W. renews his religious faith
1986	George W. quits drinking
1988	George Herbert Walker Bush elected president of the United States; George W. arranges deal to buy the Texas Rangers
1991	The Persian Gulf War starts on January 17 and ends on February 28
1994	George W. elected governor of Texas
1998	George W. reelected as governor
2000	George W. runs for president against Democrat Al Gore; November 7 election does not produce a clear winner; Supreme Court decision of December 12 hands Bush the presidency
2001	Congress approves Bush's $1.35 trillion tax-cut package on May 26; al-Qaeda terrorists attack the United States on September 11; U.S. launches air strikes in Afghanistan on October 7; Congress passes the Patriot Act on October 24; Taliban surrenders on December 6
2002	Bush signs education reform law on January 8; he speaks to UN General Assembly on September 12; UN Security Council passes resolution calling for Iraq weapons inspections on November 8
2003	Secretary of State Colin Powell addresses UN Security Council on February 5; Iraq War begins on March 19; U.S. forces seize Baghdad on April 9; Bush announces end of major combat in Iraq on May 1; Saddam Hussein arrested on December 13
2004	George W. Bush begins campaigning for reelection

GLOSSARY

al-Qaeda—radical Islamic network headed by Osama bin Laden and resolved to carry out terrorist acts against the United States and its allies.

Antiballistic Missile Treaty (1972)—treaty between the United States and the Soviet Union limiting defensive missile systems that target incoming intercontinental missiles.

Camp David—Maryland retreat northwest of Washington, D.C., used by the president of the United States.

communist—person who supports a system of government in which one group has power and property is owned by the government or community as a whole.

Democrat—older of the two major political parties of the United States concerned with broad social reform and internationalism.

derrick—structure placed over an oil well that is used to raise and lower drilling equipment.

draft—system for or act of choosing men eighteen years or older to serve forced military time during a war.

guerrillas—group that stages surprise, harassing attacks, not usual warfare.

impeach—to formally charge a public official with misconduct in office.

inauguration—ceremonial swearing in of an official into office, most often a president.

incumbent—official who currently holds a political office.

Islam—religious faith of Muslims, based on the belief that Allah is the only god and that Muhammad is his prophet.

legislature—group with the official power to make laws for a country or state.

Kurds—fourth largest ethnic group in the Middle East. They live in Northern Iraq, Iran, and central and southern Turkey.

National Convention—meeting held by one of the two major U.S. political parties to select that party's candidates for the upcoming presidential elections.

Pentagon—five-sided building that serves as the headquarters of the United States Department of Defense.

Republican—more traditional of the two major political parties of the United States.

segregation—the practice of separating people of different races, classes, or ethnic groups, especially as a form of discrimination.

Shiite Muslims—members of a branch of Islam that makes up 60 percent of Iraq's Muslims. Shiites regard Muhammad's son-in-law Ali as his legitimate successor, and only consider men from Muhammad's family as legitimate religious leaders.

Special Forces—division of the United States Army that is specially trained for independent missions and unconventional fighting techniques.

State of the Union Address—annual speech a president delivers to Congress concerning the condition of the nation as a whole.

Taliban—civilian army with some military training that follow a strict practice of Islam and took over Afghanistan in 1995.

teach-in—extended session (as on a college campus) for lectures and discussion on an important and usually controversial issue.

terrorism—use of violence, terror, and intimidation to promote fear and intimidate governments and populations.

United Nations—international organization founded in 1945 to help maintain peace between nations.

U.S. Supreme Court—highest court in the United States, consisting of nine justices.

weapons of mass destruction—nuclear, chemical, and biological weapons that may be used to harm large numbers of people over a wide area.

Vietnam War—long military conflict (1954–1975) between North Vietnam, supported by China and the Soviet Union; and South Vietnam, supported by the U.S.

FURTHER INFORMATION

Further Reading

Frank, Mitch. *Understanding September 11: Answering Questions About the Attack on America.* NY: Viking Children's Books, 2002.

Gormley, Beatrice. *First Ladies: Women Who Called the White House Home.* Madison, WI: Turtleback Books, 2004.

Gormley, Beatrice. *Laura Bush: America's First Lady.* NY: Aladdin, 2003.

Gormley, Beatrice. *President George W. Bush: Our Forty-Third President.* NY: Aladdin, 2001.

Hampton, Wilborn. *September 11, 2001: Attack on New York City: Interviews and Accounts.* Cambridge, MA: Candlewick, 2003.

Jones, Veda B. *George W. Bush.* NY: Chelsea House, 2002.

Kachurek, Sandra J. *George W. Bush.* Berkeley Heights, NJ: Enslow Publishers, 2004.

McNeese, Tim. *George W. Bush: First President of the New Century.* Greensboro, NC: Morgan Reynolds, 2002.

Meltzer, Milton. *The Day the Sky Fell: A History of Terrorism.* NY: Random House, 2002.

Miller, Debra A. *The War against Iraq.* San Diego, CA: Lucent Books, 2004.

The New York Times: A Nation Challenged, Young Readers Edition. By Staff of the NY Times. NY: Scholastic Reference, 2002.

Schlesinger, Arthur M., Jr., Fred L. Israel, and Jonathan H. Mann, eds. *The Election of 2000 and the Administration of George W. Bush.* Broomall, PA: Mason Crest, 2003.

Stewart, Gail B. *America Under Attack.* San Diego, CA: Lucent Books, 2002.

Stone, Tanya Lee. *Laura Welch Bush, First Lady.* Brookfield, CT: Millbrook, 2001.

Wukovitts, John F. *George W. Bush.* San Diego, CA: Lucent Books, 2000.

FURTHER INFORMATION

Places to Visit

George H. W. Bush Presidential
Library and Museum
1000 George Bush Drive West
College Station, TX 77845
(979) 691-4000

National Archives
700 Pennsylvania Avenue., N.W.
Washington, D.C. 20408
(866) 325-7208

The National First Ladies' Library
Education and Research Center
205 Market Avenue South
Canton, OH 44702
(330) 452-0876

Smithsonian National Museum of
American History
14th St. and Constitution Ave. N.W.
Washington, D.C. 20013
(202) 633-1000

White House
1600 Pennsylvania Avenue, N.W.
Washington, D.C. 20500
(202) 456-2121

United States Capitol
Constitution Avenue
Washington, D.C. 20515
(202) 224-3121

Web Sites

George H. W. Bush Presidential
Library and Museum
www.bushlibrary.tamu.edu

George W. Bush reelection web site
www.georgewbush.com

The National First Ladies' Library
www.firstladies.org

War on terrorism resource guide
personal.ecu.edu/durantd/wot/
index.html

The White House
www.whitehousekids.gov

INDEX

Page numbers in **bold** represent photographs.

About the Author

Ruth Ashby has written many award-winning biographies and nonfiction books for children, including *Herstory*, *The Elizabethan Age*, and *Pteranodon: The Life Story of a Pterosaur*. She lives on Long Island with her husband, daughter, and dog, Nubby.